DOCUMENTARIES

poems

WALTER HILDEBRANDT

For Tom and the wonderful Dylan Thomas song with appreciation [signature]

NEWEST PRESS
EDMONTON, AB
APRIL 2016

walter.h.hildebrandt@gmail.com

Library and Archives Canada Cataloguing in Publication

Hildebrandt, Walter, author
Documentaries / Walter Hildebrandt.
Poems.
ISBN 978-1-926455-56-3 (paperback)
I. Title.
PS8565.I4335D63 2016   C811'.54   C2015-90   6572-0

Cover image: "Captured Sioux Indians in fenced enclosure on Minnesota River below Fort Snelling" by Benjamin Franklin Upton, 1862
Board Editor: Don Kerr
Book design: Kate Hargreaves, CorusKate Design
Author photo: Ron Yaciuk

Excerpt from "Populist Manifesto No. 1" Copyright © 1976 by Lawrence Ferlinghetti. Reprinted by permission of Lawrence Ferlinghetti.

"Sisters of Mercy" Excerpted from *Stranger Music: Selected Poems and Songs* by Leonard Cohen. Copyright © Leonard Cohen. Reprinted by permission of McClelland & Stewart, a division of Random House of Canada Limited, a Penguin Random House Company.

 access© Alberta▮ Edmonton Government arts council

NeWest Press acknowledges the support of the Canada Council for the Arts, the Alberta Foundation for the Arts, and the Edmonton Arts Council for support of our publishing program. This project is funded in part by the Government of Canada.

NeWest Press

201, 8540 – 109 Street
Edmonton, AB   T6G 1E6
780.432.9427
www.newestpress.com

No bison were harmed in the making of this book.

Printed and bound in Canada

CONTENTS

To Mary—for walking Deptford and New Cross with me

There are deeper strata of truth in cinema, and there is such a thing as poetic, ecstatic truth. It is mysterious and elusive, and can be reached only through fabrication and imagination and stylization.

Werner Herzog

Our entire sense of reality has been called into question. But I do not want to dwell on this fact any longer, since what moves me has never been reality, but a question that lies behind it [beyond; dahinter]: the question of truth. Sometimes facts so exceed our expectations—that they seem unbelievable.

Werner Herzog

Give us adequate images. We lack adequate images. Our civilization does not have adequate images. And I think a civilization is doomed or is going to die out like dinossaurs if it doesn't develop an adequate language for adquate images.

Werner Herzog

ILLEGAL COMBINATIONS: GLASGOW 1787

an early blast

    fissure

        techtonic shift

            gap

1787 Glasgow Green

    beginning

        of the movement

            industrialism

against the agrarian backdrop

    and Highland removals

Glasgow Green

    the people's park

        this place of mass protests

            public demonstrations

                weaving paramount

some make as much as £100 a year

                good wages

on the heels of the collapse

            of the tobacco trade

        before the French Revolution

mechanization

    reduces workers' wages

industrial processes

    threaten

        craft–based work

    we walk the streets

of this great city

    from Gorbals to Calton to Bridgeton

city sectioned off—checkerboarded

    Gorbals grew

        a self-sufficient community

people buying from each other

    survival

    Glasgow giving birth

        to the industrial working classes

    first from tobacco sugar cotton

capital flows in

    enormous profits

        then shipbuilding and steel production

    but at the cost of polluting dyes

Sarah's grandfather

        told the story

if you swam in the Clyde

        you did not know what colour

                your skin might turn

dyes and politics

        Clyde area shading into Red Clydeside

           Irish ghettoes

              famine and marginalization

    Robbie Burns

        words

          on the street

"for all that and all that"

             poetry inscribed

               on the ground

      Above Gallowgate:

*The animals come from
over the horizon: they
were both mortal and
immortal.*

Necropolis looms over all

        see it from the Irish slums

    at a Protestant pub

      I'm told

             to take off my green pin

              from Baird's pub

here at Seven Corners

      we find the address

    of Sarah's people —the Munns

      here in the heart

           of working–class Glasgow

as immigrants to Canada they tried to hide

      how working-class they were

wanting new beginnings

        they could still taste the blood

             of conflict

the Munns buried the dead of the working-class Glasgow

their first funeral home the Calton Funeral Office

          on Abercromby Street

      where the Martyrs Monument stands

        reminder of the weavers shot

          on the Green

the Angel of History

      touched down here in Glasgow

saw the tremors

        witnessed the quake

here another history began

        Benjamin's history haunts

          these moments

            when histories start

        where you see dissensus

    disjunction

the shift

    realize the moment

      stratigraphy riven

          clear fault lines exposed

connect

    the new fault lines

      in geological time

        times that matter

            slippages

      the clear careful layered past

      disrupted

thrown-off

      thrown out

          lines altered

no longer fitting

      matching

            ground moved forever

At Glasgow Green

      walk into that past

smell the bleach

        at Seven Corners

hear the crowds

          at Drygate Bridge

      bullets

found three weavers

      shot dead

          by 39th Regiment of Foot

      whirr of the looms

highly–skilled workers

        paid well

forced

    to work overtime

      see wages adjusted

        to company–controlled standards

east of Glasgow

        large communities

   of hand-loom weavers

          weaving profitable

"a better than average lifestyle"

    many weavers well-educated

      self-taught

           a common consciousness grew

      class consciousness

   angered authorities for

           radical views

by the end of the eighteenth century

twenty thousand prosperous weavers

some owners exploit this large number

of weavers

and fed work

to those willing

to take lower wages

competition increases

capitalists look for greater profits

in Calton & Bridgeton

negotiated their prices

pick up cloth or "work"

returned it to manufacturers

in smaller outlying settlements

manufacturers cover the price of transport

undercut established weavers

Glasgow textile mills

        expand to nearly twenty

    communities grow forty percent

      wealthy owners build communities

       large homes across the Clyde

greed feeds on demand

        greater and greater

              profits

           rents

        real estate

    across the river

the building spree continues

   wage gap grows

       workers increasingly live in slums

          no sewage

            lighting

competition

        exploitation

generating

            huge profits

East India Company

        begins to import

cheaper muslin cloth

           forcing down wages

lower and lower

once thriving Glasgow communities

                ignored

working Glaswegians pushed

            to starvation

on September 3, seven thousand gather at the Green

strike

demand a just solution

companies lock them out

call in police and military

desperate times

unarmed protesters

asking to talk

answered by force

a few weavers

capitulate

work for starvation wages

strike breakers

looms are smashed in anger

the crowd unarmed

chased out of Calton by 39th Regiment of Foot

to Glasgow Green

driven out of town

regrouping

the crowd begins to return

on the edge of town

the authorities

open fire

three dead three die later

a union movement born

a moment etched in memory

Glasgow becomes home

to radical reform movements

weavers

will strike again in 1812

as repression fails

seven strikers go to jail

John Grainger tried for "forming illegal combinations"

"rent strikes" in 1915

1919 work–week strikes

Calton a burying ground for workers

unmarked "lairs" no headstones

Red Clydeside

I return to Benjamin

                    contemplating history

to destroy Whiggish misconceptions

                    his history "for" the past

"for" the future

                    in the present

                         now time

his history "for" these moments

                    moments exploding time

                         moments of recognition

                              moments to connect

                                   new communities

                    illegal combinations

LET THEM EAT GRASS / THE DAKOTA WARS 1862

Little Crow had said

    when men are hungry

        they help themselves

  warehouses with supplies and food

      ordered closed

          to hunters

Myrick at the Agency had said

    Let them eat grass

        or their own dung

Myrick's house attacked first

  found with grass

      stuffed in his mouth

    this was how they found his relative Quinn

        at Frog Lake

  who had told the starving Cree there

    that they too could eat grass

Grass

women at Fort Ripley had said

The grasses had come alive

prairie seemed to move

as the Dakota warriors

with grass bunches tied

to their headdresses

advanced

ground trembling

hair of the earth

shifting

moving

waving

Treaties

    had been

        the hope for both

           and as the ground moved

               the rules changed

        to share the land

    to make profits

        exchange/removal

           coexistence/genocide

      a better life or profits

peaceful coexistence/army removals

    either/or

    (trying) and/but

        (returning) civilization/savagery

    either/or

        need for cultural conformity

replacing the peaceful and successful

        the Dakota had lived peacefully

           next to newcomers

           for a long time

So many windows

        onto these events

     like the windows Marx

         opened onto capitalism

hard to see it all at once

       but to be seen through the many

       views

         windows

           perspectives

never just one main reason

     many causes

        built up grievances

like the Civil War

     a chance

      for Lincoln

        an advantage

          an upper hand

       hunters

subverting government initiatives

    farming   settling   colonization

      "the blanket Indians"

        those willing to farm

         to please authorities

Thirty-eight hanged

before Lincoln's re–election

largest mass hanging

popular

retribution

revenge

feared

the Dakota

as many as leaves on a tree

Red Legs

Grey Bird

Big Eagle

crawled through the grass

decoyed

many fought reluctantly

many died

at Birch Coulee

twenty men

ninety horses die

at Fort Ridgley

one hundred Dakota

twenty settlers die

Treaties and agriculture

                a way out

       treaties 1851 and 1858

                     "show" reserves

         for visiting dignitaries

       then delayed payments

provoke

       this civil war

James Lind

       hated and shot

                for abandoning his Dakota wife

then taking another

      all the resentments of the hunters

        the personal

          the political

            the cultural

              the long term

              the short term

Herzog should have made this documentary

      ironies

         complexities

             intolerance

                racism

only now the windows

        opening to some understanding

            most ironic of all

     the Dakota

        with old traditions

    of agricultural successes

           melons

       corn

    potatoes

  beans

pumpkins

   clashing in the emerging

        industrial North

   victors in the Civil War

lumping the Dakota

    with the Confederates as the defeated

  harassments

       exiles

         removals

  concentration camps

     scorched earth

       hangings

many fled to Canada

    across the Medicine Line

        refugees to the protection

            of the Queen

                once an ally

        Oak River—Sioux Valley
        Pipestone
        Bird Tail Creek
        Dakota Tipi
        Standing Buffalo
        Wahpeton
        White Cap

            all across

Saskatchewan and Manitoba

        relegated

            as non-treaty

                to small reserves

    by the 1870s some return

            to homelands

        never treated as prisoners of war

                but as criminals

the pathetic story of Little Crow

        hounded

        harassed

            shot like an animal

                displayed as a trophy

removals to

Nebraska

Montevideo

impoverished until casinos

Herzog might have liked

the huge irony

of the New Ulm

Germans

refugees from 1848

European revolutionaries

given asylum

new starts

here in Dakota country

when the fighting began

Dakota besieged

these once-revolutionary Germans

in 1862 these Dakota

refused rations

live without supplies

refused

annuity payments

witnessing the new worth of the land

land values

exchange values

the new private property

shift from fur–trading times

dissolution of kinships

imposed

by Rangers

supremacists

should have been prisoners

for the firecrackers shoved in Little Crow's ears

and exploded in his corpse

atrocities followed

desecrations

bodies disinterred

Dr. William Mayo

used them

clinical dissection

bodies returned

a century later

by the Mayo clinic

for reburial

finally the great hope

        treaties had promised

    those who could ignore them

           did the damage

those who could take prisoners

    those with the fire power

      those who could constitute "the enemy"

       those who built the scaffolds

  the treaty became a gun

       guns and gallows

for long–standing reciprocal friendship and trade

    dispersals and punishments

      war crimes

        ethnic cleansing

amnesia

       for decades

            restitution

                     that never came

  removals

      legislated violence

             humiliations

                   marginalization

            loss of homelands

    windows

        onto this complex

            history

               documentaries

WINNIPEG 1919

The true site of pleasure,
as men's primary dimension,
is neither precise, continuous
time nor eternity, but history.

Giorgio Agamben
Infancy and History

The one thing that has hurt
me possibly more than
anything else in this case
has been the display of
ignorance that I find among
men of the legal profession.

W. A. Pritchard
W.A. Pritchard's address to the jury

Nothing is so terrifying to the
Socialists of today as the folly
of their opponents.

G.B. Shaw
quoted in *W.A. Pritchard's address to the jury*

Winnipeg divided

                    now as then

               working class in the north

          business elite in the south

the Red

          running north

                    splitting the city again east from west

                              many workers saw

                    the direct link

          between the Imperium and the war

European unionists

               familiar with Marx Engels Lenin

                                   the social gospel

                    opposed

          the businessmen

                              Masons

                    Protestants

     self-made men

                         industrialists

          profiting

from the arms race

               peacetime

the time in between

      wars

           had shown them

          the military-industrial complex

Krupp and Creuset together

                  manufacturing

           advocating

an enemy at the gates

               to confiscate

      their properties

           Jews   to blame

                  the Rothchilds

             huge profits

      markets outgrowing the nation state

10 million dead

        on the battlefields of Europe

these strikers

    made history

took positions

    made agreements

        had shed the church

    marched

    against corruption and greed

revolted against the bureaucrats

    refused

        the past

          to make a better future

exploding

     the continuum of history

          disrupting

       the evolutionary

        march

              of progress

       shattering

         the established account

   making

       a new time

        a faster time

             speeding up time

politicians had said a war was needed

              a fast war

to clear the air

workers/soldiers

returning

a business elite

Citizens of One Thousand

ban

marches collective bargaining

censor

socialist classics foreign newspapers

the *Origin of Species*

blame

the foreigner

discourage

dissent

deport

        Jews and Eastern Europeans

      charge

         unionists

           beat

              protesters

           smear

      the labour movement

    criminalize

      communists

imprison

    leaders

      charge

         on horses

    refuse to bargain

         a divided city

      lines drawn

railway lines of the CPR

north from south

N   Douglas Burrows Kildonon
     Weston St. John's Inkster
     Elmwood Sargeant

S   Osborne River Heights
     Tuxedo Grant Park Riverview
     Assiniboine Wellington Crescent Heights

May 15

    a strike is called

       amid high unemployment

             soldiers returning

        businessmen

      grown rich on war

           profits

      labour's wages

        fell behind

scandals

      the Ross rifle

        Flavelle affair

          rotten hay

             shipped to armed forces

    strikes across the country

         over union recognition

  profiteering

      unemployment

Victoria Vancouver Edmonton

Calgary Prince Albert

Saskatoon Brandon

Meighen supported the Winnipeg business leaders

would not meet with labour

blamed

Bolsheviks

that "alien scum"

legislation enacted

to deport troublemakers

eradicate

the cancer

post-war patriotism

    Adorno's identity thinking

        entrenched

    a repressed middle class

      subject to a paranoia

          "they are after us"

      categorize

      patriots/foreigners

J. S. Woodsworth warned about

      Strangers Within Our Gates

   newspaper headlines

      TO HELL WITH THE ALIEN ENEMY

Bloody Sunday June 21, 1919

        6,000 veterans

     protest in a march

       close to Portage and Main

   Mayor Gray had once again

     banned all parades

       the protest and march

          peaceful

  many of the police specials

       are forgers burglars criminals

many brought in across the border from Minnesota

     Royal North-West Police

       on horses

   some have trouble controlling their mounts

the police charge

        galloping into the crowd

swinging baseball bats

transfer their bats

to their left hands

deliberately

draw guns

        and fire into the crowd

three volleys

spectators are hit

two men die

Mike Sokolowski and Steve Schezerbanoes

fighting continues down Market and James

"Hell's Alley"

        twenty-seven casualties

ninety-four arrests

(including four women)

by four in the afternoon it is over

the final charge

fueled by class fear and class hatred

Meighen and Gray

blamed the Bolsheviks

sedition

    the allegation

      unpatriotic

        the accusation

          seditious conspiracy

            the charge

in response to the attempt to gain the right to

            collective bargaining

seditious conspiracy

    to incite discontent

to incite ill will between the classes

          the King's subjects

      create public disturbances

    provoke civil war

hate of the Sovereign

      government

to incite people to unlawful associations assemblies insurrections

      breaches of the peace

conspirators charged

        all of British origin

                taken to Stony Mountain Penitentiary

Robert Russell—2 years

        he had said "Capitalism has come
        to a point where she is defunct and
        must come to an end"

William Ivens—1 year

        Methodist ministerial candidate
        expelled from the ministry for
        refusing to accept church authority

Roger Bray—6 months

        Methodist lay preacher and socialist
        who said "Christianity was
        not the means for correcting
        social injustice"

George Armstrong—2 years

        organized the Carpenters Union
        and was a founding member of the
        Socialist Party of Canada

Richard Johns—1 year

        OBU leader who said at his trial
        "I am a Socialist and
        proud of it"

William Pritchard—1 year

        athletic musical and extremely well read
        an outstanding speaker at

his trial his speech to the jury a
famous illustration of working-class
oratory

John Queen—1 year

co-founder of the Winnipeg
Socialist Sunday School

A. A. Heeps—acquitted
a pacifist who opposed conscription

immigration tribunals

Moses Almazoff—left Canada voluntarily

studied economics and philosophy

Oscar Chopperlrie—deported

authorities found "irregularities"

in his papers

these men studied

philosophy economics politics theology

more thoughtful

than the captains of industry

in their aftermath

laissez faire

given free rein again

for fifteen years

the time between wars

nationalisms grew

profits

colonies

empires continued

a precise and homogeneous continuum

of the passage of time prevailed

in the national narratives

steady progress

chronological ticking

of the clock

decades later

strikers' version of events

emerged

over time their views

vindicated

yet for a moment in 1919

    the dull time line of Whiggish history broken

      for a moment

            for a flash

                    right and left

    stood still in stark contrast

      strike leaders had said

           and history eventually showed

      they stood against

the same "band of boodlers"

    who had plundered the province

      during the war

          brought it to the verge

              of bankruptcy

for a moment in 1919

     their hegemony challenged

       unmasking

           vice and greed of capital

as Benjamin might have seen it

       a precise and homogenous

           continuum

             disrupted

    a new and revolutionary time

            emerged

       a time fulfilled

a new time full

       time of the workers

     the past refused

       the slow tick-tock of the time in between

the blur of revolutionary time

     the breakup of the homogenous time of Chronos

The Trial

    charges

       bizarre

          nightmarish

   . seditious conspiracy

W. A. Pritchard

    longshoreman

from Vancouver

   self-educated

    well-read

across many fields

    responds

asks

    what the conspiracy

where the sedition

    where did he preach hatred among men

incite discontent

preach hatred and contempt of the Sovereign

    or incite men to unlawful combinations

      associations

        insurrections

The Crown

    concocts a crazy quilt

        words deliberately misconstrued

            sentences wrenched from context

The Crown called

        Pritchard an irreligious man

Pritchard called

    the charges hateful

        a concocted poison

            a willful misrepresentation

The Crown

    compared him to an evil

        burglar arriving in the dead of the night

The Crown had agents

    entering homes of working men

        taking books papers pamphlets newspapers

            snipping out sections

to show evidence of sedition

      books were taken from Pritchard's home

            many of them his father's

         with a surgical knife they carved out terms

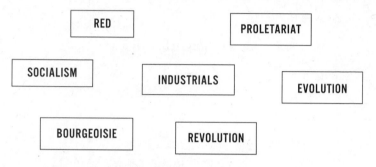

little pieces of poison

      Eureka Eureka

         the Crown

   mix it all up

      find it

            seditious

    this collection of

      words

     sentences

         utterances

        independent of each other

   gathered together

     like a farmer taking eggs

  from different nests

putting them in one basket

and calling it "seditious conspiracy"

                              is how Pritchard put it

        they took all those bits

                they thought damaging

                left out

        what could exonerate

Pritchard begins

        to unmix the concoction

     tells the judge and jury

          education is not sedition

     tells them what he believes

            believes in

              ultimately

        the union of the workers

    will bring peace to the world

Pritchard addresses the jury

      on two main issues

he tells them

free enterprise is unsustainable

there has been profiteering

in the capitalist system

labour lives in miserable conditions

the proletariat thinly clothed

poorly paid

barely housed

exhausted from excessive

and repetitive work

buffeted by ever rising prices

raises in rent

that production is for profit

not for use

workers alienated

from the products

they produce

they are increasingly becoming

mere unskilled labourers

that the working class

has little to combat this onslaught

inflation

crises in overproduction

    resulting unemployment

        layoffs

  poor working condition

  they need to organize

      to unite

          form unions

starting in 1799 with combinations

eventually a union movement

legitimized

with 1908 legislation

workers also believe

in production for use

not for profit

to end impoverishment

of the working man

Pritchard tells them

        socialism

           is born

      from the working class

   wanting to free itself from

                 the bourgeoisie

trade unions

    formed

       to combat

the changes wrought by the machine

    the decline of craft-based unions

workers divorced from their tools

        workers with little security

           against the vagaries of

                unemployment

     declining wages

       need decent working hours

             a minimum wage

with capital

  constantly

     attacking

        undermining

           their combinations

       organizations

   unions

political parties

Pritchard tells the judge and jury

    that the present party system

        is class based

corrupted by class interests

    that all the world's resources

        lie in the hands

          of oligarchies

    profiteering

  during the war

Pritchard describes

  this crowd

    of noisome flies

      fattening at a carcass

sent soldiers to the field in boots

        that fell apart

           soldiers had to tie

      shingles and wood

    to their boots

      to keep their soles

        off the ground

    party politics

that stinks in the nostrils

      of all honest men

Pritchard tells them

        why he admires Marx

     why the *Communist Manifesto*

               is an important history

        of the evolution

                of the working class

      from medieval times

          to the present

           the history

               of the working class

     is indeed the history of class warfare

Pritchard tells them

      that Marx wrote

   men do not make movements

        movements make men

Pritchard tells them

    that working people

        and trade unionists

            horrified

    by the War Measures Act

          the resulting censorship of many

                  scientific books
silencing trade unionists

          outlawing ideas

    what they banned revealed "unadulterated ignorance"

          democracy can mask dictatorship

Pritchard

    gives them a history lesson

        on the meaning of "revolution"

Pritchard tells them

    trade unionists

        worked hard to gain

            concessions through parliamentary action

        pursuing power by the vote

            running candidates

Pritchard quotes from many sources

            sometimes by memory

            Toynbee
            Gibbon
            Shaw
            Lenin
            Galileo
            Anatole France

he anticipates Althusser's

        sociological insights

                the workings of social controls

                        showing how

       protestantism capitalism imperialism

                            intertwine

          lessons in economics and unemployment

a command performance

        in telling the judge

           how he reasons

        unlike the judge

       he has a different "habit of thought"

Pritchard tells the judge

        his legal mind

              is an

          "indoor mind"

    and the indoor mind

          does not understand

              the outside world

  that Pritchard as a working man

          of necessity

      must be aware of the big picture

  the political economy

        he lives in

lawyers like to keep things as they are

      not aware of big world movements

          shaking men out of their slumber

socialists trade unionists

are changing things to make the world

a better place to live

in contrast

to the Crown

fearing the OBU

as a danger to their commercial system

lawyers have their fair share

of the good things in life

the plutocracy

likes to preserve the status quo

cannot see why anyone is discontent

why there should be unrest

can't understand people living in bondage

prices going up

wages going down

Pritchard tells them he cannot hire a lawyer

                to argue for him

      that against the judge's advice

            he defends himself

         does not think like a lawyer

     narrowly

the Crown claims

    Pritchard preached class hatred

             advocated violence

    Pritchard says he preached understanding

                not hate

       education

              not ignorance

      industrial peace

             not violence

Pritchard claims

      he is being convicted by spies

          maliciously lying

             misrepresenting

                all he stands for

Pritchard says he has the right

          to advocate for alternative politics

      he says nothing more or worse

          than what is in the

             Manchester Guardian

            or other press

                in the United Kingdom

Pritchard asked

what can you do

if your bosses

do not obey the labour laws of the country

when politicians

will not speak

for working people

and the laws to protect them

laws won by the trade union movement

passed by Parliament

working people driven into a corner

working people slandered by the press

owned by the business elites

Pritchard exasperated tells the court

> *I have met coal miners from the*
> *face of the rock who would argue*
> *points in philosophy and political*
> *economy as well as anyone I have*
> *ever heard. I think honestly, in my*
> *own mind that some of these scarred*
> *black-faced toilers from the depths*
> *of mines could write better editorials*
> *with their picks possibly than the*
> *editor of the 'Free Press' with his pen.*

the Crown accuses Pritchard

of class hatred

Pritchard explains to the court

what the Socialist Party identifies as

the dictatorship of the bourgeoisie

that his party advocates

the suppression of

the dictatorship of

the financers
the profiteers
the Flavelles
the Rosses
the Allisons

unscrupulous Wall Street financers

foreign and Canadian

Pritchard asks the court again and again

where was the criminal intent

or maliciousness

what was damaging

(surely not his father's books)

or literature on

industrial depressions

commercial crises

the crisis of overproduction

rises in the cost of living

Is this sedition Pritchard asks

Pritchard claims finally and in summation

        the Crown's argument so weak

                against him

they resorted to creating a bogeyman

      a kilamazoo

          something that never existed

            something entirely false

picking and choosing

      what they thought damaging

        leaving everything else out

          a personal assassination

and in the end

    Pritchard

      places faith in history

        some eventual redemption

          vindication

*. . . and in my own mind I rest
assured that the historian of the
future will drive the knife of critical
research into the very bowels of the
bogey that has been conjured forth out
of the imagination of certain legal
luminaries of this city*

EDMONTON 2012

Oh the sisters of mercy, they are not departed or gone.
They were waiting for me when I thought that I just can't go on.
And they brought me their comfort, and later they brought me this song.
Oh I hope you run into them, you who've been traveling so long.

When I left they were sleeping, I hope you run into them soon.
Don't turn on the lights, you can read their address by the moon.
And you won't make me jealous if I hear that they sweetened your night:
We weren't lovers like that, and besides it would still be all right,
We weren't lovers like that, and besides it would still be all right.

Leonard Cohen
"The Sisters of Mercy"
Stranger Music: Selected Poems and Songs

Poets, come out of your closets,
Open your mind and, open your doors.
You have been holed-up too long
In your closed worlds.

Lawrence Ferlinghetti
San Francisco Poems

THE NOT ALWAYS ALREADY

I take the long way

    each day to drive down the riverbank

       a dream world compressed

         in fragments

      an ancient waterway

        burial sites

            place of forts

banks lush green in the summer

   dazzlingly white in winter

steep banks

    deep and dark waters

        dangerous currents

on my descent

      into this magnificent valley

I'm haunted

    by what this city is built on

Papaschase

without a reserve

from 1877 when he was to sign the treaty

to 1898 when an agreement

he had not signed was handed to him

fraudulent surrender

orchestrated

by newcomers

police

government officials

newspapers

politicians

clergy

community leaders

open season on Papaschase

a chief who had resisted

conversion

who (unlike many chiefs around him)

had not become a Christian

Frank Oliver

Ontarian

who hated his father

changes his family name

founder of the *Edmonton Bulletin*

claimed Papaschase not a "real Indian"

their land needed by incoming settlers

people who paid taxes

in response to a dispute

Indian Agent Inspector Wadsworth

arbitrarily

reduced the size of Papaschase's band

by signing eighty-four of them onto the list

the "Edmonton Stragglers"

divide and conquer

complemented by reports in the *Bulletin*

a campaign to portray Papaschase

as a foreigner

Indians not from around here

    (as if Oliver was *from around here*)

        justifying removal

    newcomers did not want Edmonton

                encircled by Indians

1885 Papaschase's people

      offered scrip

          devious and pernicious

      pieces of paper

          death of a people by paper

    a starving people

who could not read or write English

      who could not make an informed decision

    lost their treaty rights

            homeless still

      a few dollars in their hands

        paper genocide

for whom no reserve had been surveyed

Inspector Wadsworth embarked on attempts

to lure Papaschase's people into a land surrender

no official meeting held

no quorum present

three people found who would sign

though eight were legally required

Papaschase's people eventually disperse

without anything

early story of Edmonton

refuse reserves

where the CPR might run

away from what was already settled

paradise for speculators

no Aboriginal people

to encounter

to bargain with

or confront

(in a remarkable footnote

the Reverend John McDougall

a leader in the anti-Papaschase movement

sought to buy the Aboriginal and Métis lands

after they were surrendered and

opened up to surveyors)

a century later

      the Supreme Court of Canada invokes

the statue of limitations

      rules that descendants of Papaschase cannot

            pursue their claim

We cannot speculate on evidence that

      might be heard in the future

later one newspaper reads

      Land illegally taken . . . a reserve disbanded

         . . . given to white settlers

Cree lawyer Ron Maurice said

The story should have been

one of opportunity and wealth.

Instead what you see

are a people looking in

Gerhard Ens

historian for the Crown opined

federal authorities at the time

may have made

inappropriate decisions

Fort Edmonton

      outpost of Empire

         Europe extends its reach

            further into North America

               trading on the edge

               beaver skins for top hats

                    fashionable in Europe

    a network fanning out

         from the Bay to the Pacific

                  posts and factors

eager for

>beaver skins
>lynx marten wolf
>muskrat otter mink
>fox bear buffalo

willing to trade

>guns ammunition
>tools utensils
>European cloth
>blankets jewellery
>spices liquor
>traps

Fort Edmonton at the centre

of a major commercial network

Peace River   York Factory

Norway House

Hudson Bay

Cypress Hills

labourers at the post treated harshly

backbreaking work

miserly pay

in spring York boats make the trip to Norway House

with furs for Europe

travel three months with the current

harder on the return upstream

men who falter or waiver

beaten

mutinies ensue

factors Rowand and Hardisty

        pinching pennies

    company profits to shareholders grow

           at the expense

     of Métis labourers

      missionaries come and go

       clergy trying

to convert Métis and Cree

   their names endure

      Rundle McDougall Lacombe

         plastered

   all over the city

     on schools churches and street signs

Rowand's death celebrated

    by Métis labourers

in one incident of rebellion

    trip men throw a much–hated factor overboard

    abandon him to wilderness

Fort Edmonton

       hub of more than the fur trade

a dozen York boats built each year

          hundreds of buffalo manufactured into

pemmican

   by Métis and Cree women

       staple of the Northwest

  fuelled the fur trade

        hay cut and sold

    coal mined nearby

   hunters bring deer moose fish fowl

     to feed the fort

firewood chopped

dogs trained for sledding

   horses for freighting

       gardens cultivated

         to supply a staple

   potatoes

a gateway to the North

suppliers to the Peace Mackenzie districts

when brigades leave for Norway House much work

left to a few

outfitting Overlanders to the Pacific

gold rushes to the Caribou and Klondike

Cree and Blackfoot main traders to the fort

introduce rituals and ceremonies

gift giving

jackets and tobacco presented to the chiefs

liquor doled out

before business begins

the greatest skill of the factors

to negotiate peacefully

with diverse and sometimes

warring tribes

Cree Blackfoot Assiniboine Tsuu T'ina

traditional enemies

atmosphere tense

    when faulty trade rifles misfired

        limbs lost

    Blackfoot furious

      threaten to attack the post

Factors host events

    celebrate visitors

explorers surveyors artists government officials

      harbingers of Empire

   artist Paul Kane is served a festive meal

      mouffle
      dried moose nose
      white fish in buffalo marrow
      buffalo tongue
      beaver tails
      roast wild goose

      he writes—this is the food of our country

then a dance

the evening hall . . . filled by
gaily dressed guests. Indians
whose chief ornament consisted
in paint on their faces, voyageurs
with bright sashes and neatly
ornamented mocassins, half-breeds
glittering in every ornament
they could lay their hands on;
whether civilized or savage
all were laughing and jabbering
in as many different languages
as there were styles of dress.
English, however, was little used
as none could speak it. . . . The
dancing was most picturesque
and almost all joined in.
Occasionally I, among the rest,
led out a young Cree squaw, who
sported enough beads around
her neck to have made a
peddler's fortune, and having
led her to the centre of the
room, I danced round her
with all the agility I was
capable of exhibiting, to
some highland reel which
the fiddler played with great
vigour, whilst my partner
with grave face kept
jumping up and down, both
feet off the ground at once. . .

often partying until early morning

couples who spend the night together

prevail on the factor to declare them married

the next morning

unions with traveling voyageurs

thus sanctified

the fur trade wanes

York boats replaced by

steamboats and rail

during the 1885 Métis Resistance

Fort Edmonton aided as best it could

the North-West Mounted Police

and General Middleton's Field Force

the HBC never sympathetic

to local grievances

continues to reap profits

fruits of civil war

charging inflated prices for

livestock hay provisions

to soldiers

in pursuit of Big Bear

mixed boreal forest

a transition zone

between parkland and prairie

a favoured wintering site

in sheltering forest

rich with game

a launching place

in summer to the prairie

for the buffalo hunt

Papaschase (the woodpecker)

        himself Saulteaux and Québécois

    at once chief of an Aboriginal tribe

        and Métis freeman

            in the employ of the HBC

      as supplier and labourer

        some more European

      some more Aboriginal or Métis

all saw themselves as a community

          derisively referred to as

            The Edmonton Stragglers

Métis/the members of the Papaschase band

        in 1870 decimated by smallpox

this territory where people often fought

         against the Blackfoot Assiniboine Tsuu T'ina

iron-fisted monopoly of the HBC

       the legacy of Governor George Simpson

                so determined

           to make the fur trade

                as profitable as possible
                  his frontier capitalism

      established foundations

for racism paternalism class conflict

            reducing wages

               whenever he could

            seeking

        short-term contractors

keep costs down

     preserve the HBC monopoly

others

Michel's Chief Calliho

eventually settled in St. Albert

lost reserve land

through another one of

Oliver's illegal surrenders

of so—called unused land

orchestrated

by the corrupt

Laurier Liberals

people of this land

  not builders of Empire

    not colonizers who secretly transferred

      title to Aboriginal and Métis lands

        in a sale

    ignoring the original people of Rupertsland

  South Bank named after Lord Strathcona

        Donald Smith

    a robber baron

 who founded and funded

    Strathcona's Horse

  to fight the Boer War

Strathcona an early investor

in Middle East petroleum

before Turner Valley and Leduc

from University Avenue north to the river

originally Métis river lots

held also by Orkneymen

Garneau Walter Colin Hamelin Ward

Kipling Daigneault Bird Quinn Gauthier

post-1885 immigration

of Anglo-Protestants to Strathcona

displaces the old Métis settlement

1885 Resistance crushed

further dispossession

of the dispossessed

UNSETTLED SETTLEMENT

in Edmonton—the capital city

                home of the political

     elite

an economy lurching from crisis to crisis

             benefiting the oligarchs

     the ideas of Hayek

        Strauss

          Friedman

            Schmitt

    trickle-downers   supply-siders

    Flanagan   Morton   Cooper

    Bercuson   Knopf

teaching Reform 101

    disciples from the south

        propping up

    ideas of plutocracy

democracy threatening

    entrenched power

      only the few can understand

        filling the capital

      with fantasies

    of free enterprise

Money Money Money

    money to make the world go round

      new capital of the Oilpatch

        corporate capitalism

character assassination

disinformation

taught Harper

to ignore

opposition

deny protest

oil and gas prices

land values

labour costs

environmental disasters

crisis to crisis

enriching the few

building a link

from

Turner Valley
Leduc
Leduc 2
Athabasca Tar Sands

pipelines to the Gulf

the Pacific

over mountains

to Asia

oil to fuel

the unquenchable thirsts

of the developed world

plastics nylon rubber asphalt lubricants

land
refineries
extraction
transport
pipelines

labour imported from

Newfoundland and Africa

we see these workers

racing down Highway 2

for weekends in the bars

on Whyte Avenue

drugged and drunk

Edmonton with the highest

murder rate in Canada

workers letting off steam

after hard work

long hours

on Euclids   enormous dump trucks

money to burn

well-paid labour needed

to drive the

machines
refineries
extraction
transport
pipelines

jobs in

nanotechnologies
surface sciences
organic chemistry
molecular biology
semiconductor physics
microfabrication

a new global world

without boundaries

plutocrats

        set free to profit

   land   labour   money

          here in the capital

     democracy is hard to find

       avenues of opposition blocked

   contrary voices suppressed or dismissed

the press

   marginalized

universities

  do their own corporate funded environmental impact studies

      to tell us there is no impact

      yet

    spills are endemic to pipelines

       capitalism runneth over

    runs us over

     leaks

farmers and workers unemployed

hurting through the Depression

disillusioned with the hope first kindled

by the UFA

everyone swung to Social Credit in '35

Socreds began a long occupation

brought out latent anti-Semitism

promoted anti-alcohol campaigns

(fights for decades over whether Alberta could serve booze)

party anti-capitalist

swept the province in 1934

Bible Bill Aberhart

       passionately believing

         capitalism

             to be corrupt and immoral

     rotten materialistic

         believing

               not understanding

        the A + B theorem of Major Douglas

   promising to spend his way

out of the Depression

       everyone to get twenty-five bucks

              funny money

Bible Bill

        a radically fundamentalist Baptist

leads a mass movement of the discontent

           firmly grounded in Christian conservatism

                    motivated

        by weekly radio broadcasts

           "dispensationalism"

                    regular listeners across the West

inspirational

    an excellent high school teacher

      all agreed

        at first Aberhart

          tries to help the poor

        froze debt

began public works

      promised debt relief

        increased taxes

          reducing deficits

        health social educational

    services supported

but reforms to the monetary system

    are struck down

        ultra vires

          unconstitutional

      held the House of Lords

bills of recall press control bank reform

                      fails

          Ernest Manning

                    a Cold Warrior

                          follows Bible Bill

                 communists

     boogeymen

          everywhere

               in the union movement

      stifles   restricts   suppresses

                          workers' rights

                    censors films

           flows with oil

               rides a wave of prosperity

Manning

    reverses Aberhearts populism

        introduces

      conservative Christian fundamentalism

        entrenched til 1971

  when the Conservatives of Peter Lougheed

                succeeds socreds

       different from Aberhart and Manning

    lawyer football player Harvard MBA

              a Red Tory

the face of conservatism hardly changes

           "the Right"

     staunchly stubbornly intransigent

      then

            the emergence of ugly times

with Ralph Klein

blew up hospitals

attacked the poor

taunted the dispossessed

throwing money at them

in a drunken stupor

at the end

of a bender

Ralph

drunk on oil

ensures that

oil calls the shots

King Ralph presided over

the largest slashing of government programs

against this political backdrop

and often amidst all this

in Edmonton

HOPE CIRCLING IN THE BELLY OF THE BEAST

a few small mercies appear

John Reimer

Jan Reimer

Grant Notley

Laurence Decore

Tommy Banks

Big Miller

Rachel Notley

celebrations

The Fringe

Jazz Fest

Blues Fest

Folk Fest

women of the GWG plant

the war on the picket lines

defying Peter (Puck) Pocklington

diversity

in Edmonchuk

Redmonton

Gretzky

        moving up ice

   slowly

like some creature beaming out radar

              with the grace of a speed skater

      weaving

   dexterously criss-crossing legs

           finding speed

     turning on a dime

stopping suddenly

      behind the net

           master of all he surveys

    you know the puck

       will be in the net

   creating space for Kurri

      who out of nowhere

            bangs it home

       night after night

    enacting the same magic

      never been anything like him since

Parker

      looking up field

         before he even has the ball

knowing there's a way

          through

    all those helmets and pads

      slowly at first

           then faster towards the sidelines

    back reversing fields

          they've tried to stop him

dangling down the sidelines

    bouncing off tacklers

           his legs don't stop

    they can't find his legs

           just wet noodles

    grasp at air

        he's on his way to paydirt

        the endzone

   with Spaghetti Legs

Hec Gervais

    crouches in the hack

        unfazed by all the rocks in the rings

    nerves of steel

staring down the prospects

        the percentages

            another impossible shot

          gliding

       pushing off

   in a firm steady motion

       extending

     the last light touch

          to the inturn

straw brooms in tandem

     the rock cutting into the ice

             curling

      past the stones

like a ship into port

    past guards

       and all the granite

         to the button

            the Gentle Giant

Messier

    local boy

        tough   determined

struck fear into hearts of opponents

           an unflinching steely stare

    defying anyone to stop him

        a blistering shot

    Mess could find the smallest corner

        could fly

           down the wing

                leaving bodies

        strewn

           behind

    to the net

inspiring teammates

    intimidating

        finding ways to win

The Edmonton Grads

between 1915 and 1940

a record 502 wins to 20 losses

outlasted the opposition

superior physical conditioning

no smoking no drinking

no marrying

winning four Olympic Gold medals

Paris London Amsterdam Berlin

winning all twenty-seven games

brought out big crowds

wherever they went

best women's basketball

Canada has known

Finest basketball team

that ever stepped out

on a floor

Dr. James Naismith
Inventor of basketball

Fuhr

        unorthodox   left-handed

            athletic

     saw a lot of rubber

          through the glory years

those Oiler teams not known for defense

     often falling behind by big scores

            only to have Gretzky Kuri Anderson

            Messier Coffey

               score buckets of goals

     while Fuhr single-handedly sometimes

kept them in the game

            backstopped the team night after night

     came the stress   the demons

            pucks that flew at night

     shrugged it off

Gretzky thought him the greatest

            goaltender in NHL history

     in '87 he helped beat a tough Soviet team

            in a Canada Cup victory

Kwon

        compact tough solid quick

                a fullback hard to bring down

      durable

lasted fourteen seasons

        three Grey Cups in a row

            mastered the tough grind

          slicing through the line

              up the gut

         also renowned

            for sailing around the end

notoriously determined

        when the chips were down

ended his career holding thirty records

        remembered as

           the China Clipper

Edmonton Folk Festival

city hovers floats

in the distance

the great deep mighty

North Saskatchewan

flows quietly

below

ravens float

iridescences

shimmering in the heat

waves of warmth

and music

dirt   grit   sweat   sunscreen

smells of food waft

across the hill

10,000 jammed

        sardines

    sun blazes

          sweat pours

  thin cloth

      damp

    exposed

         midriffs

      scantily

  tight

      shorts

         sundresses

    raised above knees

x-legged

  broad

    wide open

     river valley

       side stages

         smaller gatherings

beer tents

    relief

        from heat

mosquitoes

        sometimes bad music

breasts thinly covered

      reveal

        all sorts

    of nipples

        greying "'60s" types

        paisleys

           Birkenstocks

      flowing skirts

drifting from tent to tent

        dust raised

    from sandaled feet

              onion cakes

                           pastas

      jerk chicken

                  Korean cabbage

chorizo

        Fat Franks

stage side

      ample swaying hips

          dancers

             callipygous

       arms waving

            flowing skirts

         sun

                beating down

        entranced

    worshipping

        the Blues

           Folk

       R&B

     Pop

   Rock

     Gospel

worshippers

     of sound

       lost in rhythms

   candles

     waving in the wind

          poles identifying

             territory

blue plastic 8 x 10's

marijuana

        drifts

           above the crowd

      horses on stilts

              dance to the blues

          plump red babies

            their first

                   outdoor music

music has grown up

        from this prairie place

            demanding

         this music and The Fringe

            festivals of blues and jazz

                              baseball hats

                                    muslin Tilleys

                                          cowboy

                        straw brimmed

                  berets

            Panamas

        even bowlers

pork pies

smokers

            on the edge

                  and recycling

                        the latest in recycling

      T-shirt says

            "Life's short play dirty"

        dancing

                  sunning

                        drinking

                              talking

Roger's neckerchiefs everywhere

      halter tops

   bad dress

     everywhere

here prairie people

     don't care

       about high-toned fashion

    glass reflections

     of this Lego city

       from the Muttart Conservatory

        to the Hotel Macdonald

    lit up grandly

       in the night

Ben Harper's diamonds

   downtown light

     glitters

      as evening

       descends

        into darkness

musical prisms

remain

a slower John Prine stays – reverberating

"Make me an angel

that flies

from Montgomery . . ."

music from the ground

up

a flying Angelus

rising

full of hope

and horror

LIVING IN THESE END TIMES

beginnings

    new starts

        not in this West

            of heroic individualism

                not in the mavericks

                cowboys

            traders in business and politics

            classically

        epitomizing

                Weber's Protestant

                    ethic

            devoured by greed

what could the Sisters of Mercy bring us

        a new language

    new compassion

        a contested peace

after the war

a Rudy Wiebe

or a new spring revival

in Bob Kroetsch's classic long poem

Kroetsch and Wiebe

in and of this place

Blues from the Commercial

Jazz from the Yardbird Suite

something to sweeten the night

out of all this conservative evangelism

redemptive moments

the now time

a small gateway

through

LONDON 2011

Here amid the horror of this century

I read *Living in the End Times*

and witness the terrible beating

of a young girl by a gang

of drug–crazed teenagers

on Caledonian Road

am warned

not to interfere

I'm told they

all have blades

the young girl is being kicked and punched

by boys and girls alike

with pointed boots

the girl is limp

and is dragged

across the pavement

we ask someone to call the police

traffic is crazy everywhere

             pedestrians at risk

      buses cars trucks whiz by

                 you need to be constantly alert

Londoners are anxious

        in a hurry to get by

      in this ever so expensive city

        you wonder how they get by

there is some kind of death wish

                 in this traffic

        a pent–up violence trying to get out

in some shops the service is surly

        the attitude seems to be

          oh no—not another customer

back to the frantic traffic

              jackhammers

drilling in the streets

        the violence of construction

                for the Olympics

many Londoners are angry

        over the impositions

                disruptions

back at home

    the familiar

        hockey draft

      I mail in my picks

           no *Hockey News* here

young women wear

      blue jean shorts and miniskirts

          over black stockings

at the University of London

        Sarah works in "The Senate"

            Ministry of Truth

    built in the '30s

      where 1984 was filmed

          where

George	Orwell
Dylan	Thomas
T.S.	Eliot
Virginia	Woolf
Leonard	Woolf
Maynard	Keynes

  worked at decoding

    to demoralize the enemy

at the "Angel" tube stop

a "drug dog"

sniffs

people coming up from the underground

catching a wiff

circles a young man

with the leash

astonished at what I'm seeing

the young man is taken aside

powerless

we walk the streets

in dreams

I work next to my father

against fire

and the collapsing banks

of the South Saskatchewan River

search for the "emancipatory collective"

Žižek's ideal society

Žižek's new totalities

breaking through

in this warm spring

in Green Park

women sunning

in their bras

feel free here to take

their blouses off

relax

on a postcard

      we see William and Harry

          in uniform

clearly

    defending

        our "common/wealth"

at Russell Square

    at the fountain

       a crazy mongrel dog

        barks

           in consternation

bites frantically

    at the water

       shooting up at the centre

          of the square

it's a sunny April day

        little rain and wind

                this year

    couples soak up

          this early spring sun

     talk

        embrace

lovely striped deckchairs

      adorn Green Park

   park attendants

        ask for two quid

to pay for the ones we sit in

    a kind of rent we suppose

I imagine Žižek writing

   in his office some blocks away

        black tulips bloom

         a white cross

           at their centre

CUBA JANUARY 2011

lives began here

        new moments

    in fertile crevices

          amid what's crumbling

a momentary hope

      against all odds

           a chance

              for redemption

dreaming here in Cuba

          sensuous

     ravishing

Salsa Dancers

        this place of cigars

        mojitos

           Buena Vista jazz

I want to die here

    in this place of great resistances

                to colonizers

       to the fascist Batista

    slaves

          the Americans

            of the Bay of Pigs

Here in the streets at the Havana

    where even the dogs

      lean   mangy

      run independently

      don't seek affection

   don't want to be petted

couples come here

    where the lifeguards

      all along the beaches

        know it's dangerous

DEPTFORD 2012 / MARLOWE('S) HAUNTS

For Mary then living in New Cross

Was this the face that launched a thousand ships,
And burnt the topless tower of Ilium—
Sweet Helen, make me immortal with a kiss.—
[kisses her]
Her lips suck forth my soul: see where it flies!—
Come, Helen, come give me my soul again.
Here will I dwell for heaven is in these lips,
And all is dross that is not Helena.

Christopher Marlowe
The Tragical History of the Life and Death of Doctor Faustus

Black is the badge of hell
The hell of dungeons and the school of night

William Shakespeare
Love's Labour's Lost

If religion does this to men's bodies,
then let us have no more religion.
We shall be happier without God and his
black crows of ministers. I do not forget
what was done under bloody Mary and
know it will happen again if the Spanish
take us over. It is all one, true reformed
or true papish. It is religion itself that is our
true enemy […] Cast down God like a wooden
puppet. He and his saints are only fit for oaths.

Kit Marlowe
from Anthony Burgess's
A Dead Man in Deptford

we walk from Goldsmith's

                  towards the river

          along Deptford High Street

New Vision

      African

              Hair Salon

      Halal butcher

                  Chinese variety shops

      then as now

            streets crowded with working people

chai tea houses

          where ragpickers scoured alleys

walking along the river

            The Dog and Duck pub

      below Thames mudlarks

              busy scavenging the riverside

next to the site where Francis Drake

          received his knighthood

                    from Elizabeth I

Chaucer's

      route to Canterbury

              through Deptford

passed St. Nicholas Church

where a great poet lies

unmarked

dumped

without ceremony

close to where

they conspired

plotted

this untimely

death

silence by those

with much to fear

Marlowe knew too much

his arrest immanent

an interrogation looming

Asian   African   Indian

working poor

replace

the men and women

who laboured

in and by

those shipyards

of Elizabeth I and Henry VIII

abandoned now

traces

almost gone

of those earlier

working poor

in shipyards

victualleries

where salt beef

stocked vessels

heading out across the seas

from English ports

biscuits for the entire Navy

        mustard flaking

    flour grinding

men of the large cooperage

          making barrels

    victualling yards

      covering 19 acres

among the largest in the world

    Marlowe knew their pungent stench

here girls and women

    butchered sheep and cattle

          for centuries

John Hawkins

    launched ships to Africa

        dark human cargo

           here at auction

        Olaudah Equaino

              sold

            only to rise

              to abolish slavery

  further on a great gate

        remains

      entrance to the Royal Victualling Yards

now empty Sayes Court

          where Mary reads the small plaque

  telling of Peter the Great

             who came to learn

                 shipbuilding

while being housed

for three months in 1698

at Sayes Court built by diarist John Evelyn

attracting throngs

to his magnificent gardens

Peter and his men rented the estate

went on drunken sprees

they drove the Czar

in a wheelbarrow

through the hedges

of the fine English gardens

mad drunken sailors

caused irreparable damage

to the glorious cultivated gardens

ramming through them

again and again

A Dead Man in Deptford

                              destined to die

         atheist

                 lover of all

                          beauty

         his death drive

                          a trip

                 through

                                        London

                          Cambridge

                          Deptford

                 crossing oceans

                                   to France

fist fights

                 murders

                          assassinations

                                   executions

spying

       for his Protestant Queen

              treachery

        the plots of Mary Stuart

Elizabeth's spymaster Walsingham

         hires bright young penniless students

    looking for a chance

       looking for a break

Spanish schemes

        Philip's Catholic plots

   double agents

          finally

              the Babington Plot

    snuffed out

       with the gathered intelligence

Marlowe and others

       supplied to Walsingham

Babington Ballard five others

        tried   convicted

       sentenced to death

drawn   quartered   hanged

      in such a grisly

            horror

               so gruesome

      Marlowe never forgot it

      a second group then hanged

          before being disemboweled

          then Mary too

      tried   convicted   beheaded

             bloody Mary

Marlowe for his part

        had enrolled in a seminary

            in Rheims

      preparing for the priesthood

        back home

           Marlowe

           squandered

        Elizabeth's payments

  lavish parties

      huge drinking bouts

        sumptuous meals

    such wealth

        totally unknown to him

a small cell

gathered around Raleigh

atheists—among them

George Chapman – classical scholar
Thomas Harriet – chemist
John Florio – linguist
John Dee – astrologer
Christopher Marlowe

all students

science   philosophy   religion

free thinkers

met secretly

ideas that frightened authorities

chasms between

scientific thought   church dogma

widening

intellectuals went underground

Marlowe gathered what he could

       scraps here and there

    spying for a Queen

     in France

        exposing plots

    yet in horror

       of revenge killings

he saw no great good in God

        deeds in the name of the Father

          preferred a disbelief

   not Catholic not Protestant

     active in the School of Night

          atheists

meeting

    Sir Walter Raleigh

          to read

   his thoughts

     Marlowe wrote carefully

      clandestinely

had never forgotten at age 8

the slaughter of French Huguenots

rivers running red

with blood

no God

no salvation

Marlowe's Faust

his hope to disassemble hierarchies

authority

a lingering hope in man himself

by and for himself

creator of Faust

his history

temptations

magic

denials

demonism

science against the church

good/evil

the hubris of knowledge

with Faust

    he wrote

        his own life

    dying in Deptford

        stabbed in the eye

silenced for all he knew

        like Faust he came from nothing

            son of a cobbler

        and left in ignominy

           dismembered

           by enemies

        haunting

           looming

           launching

such beauty

        amid the dismantling

        destruction

    of his administered world

        we walk back

      in and with

    a suspended

disbelief

BIBLIOGRAPHY AND NOTES

ILLEGAL COMBINATIONS: GLASGOW 1787
Dudgeon, Piers, *Our Glasgow: Memories of Life Disappearing Britain*. London:
Headline Reviewer, 2009.

LET THEM EAT GRASS/THE DAKOTA WARS 1862
Bakeman, Mary Hawker, and Antona M. Richardson, eds. *Trail of Tears:
Minnesota's Dakota Indian Exile Begins*. Roseville: Prairie Echoes, 2008.

Dahlin, Curtis A., *The Dakota Uprising: A Pictorial History*. Edina: Beavers Pond
Press, 2009.

Monjeau-Marz, Corrine L., *The Dakota Indian Interment at Fort Snelling*, 1862-
1864. St. Paul: Prairie Smoke Press, 2005.

WINNIPEG 1919
Bumstead, J.M., *Winnipeg General Strike of 1919: An Illustrated History*. Winnipeg:
Watson and Dwyer, 1996.

Pritchard, W.A., *W.A. Pritchard's Address to the Jury*. Winnipeg: Wallingford Press,
n.d.

EDMONTON 2012
MacGregor, James Grierson, *Edmonton: A History*. Edmonton: Hurtig, 1967.

Monto, Tom with Lawrence Randy, *Old Strathcona: Edmonton's Southside Roots*.
Edmonton: Crang Publishing, 2011.

Silversides, Brock, Fort de Prairies: *The Story of Fort Edmonton*. Surrey: Heritage
House, 2005.

DEPTFORD 2012/MARLOWE('S) HAUNTS
Burgess, Anthony, *A Dead Man in Deptford*. London: Vintage Books, 2010.

The quotations by Werner Herzog on page 6, are from www.wernerherzog.com/52.
html and en.wikiquote.org/wiki/werner_herzog

The quote by Gerhard Ens in "Edmonton 2012" can be found at *CBC News* posted
Feb 22, 2008.

The quote by G.B. Shaw in "Winnipeg 1919" can be found in *W.A. Pritchard's Address to the Jury*

ACKNOWLEDGEMENTS

Sarah Carter, Mary Hildebrandt, Rosie Pucci, Segiy Kozokov, Charles Noble, Don
Kerr, Jenna Butler

Historian and poet **WALTER HILDEBRANDT** was born in Brooks, Alberta and now lives in Edmonton. He was the Director of University of Calgary Press and Athabasca University Press. He has worked as a historian for Parks Canada and as a consultant to the Treaty 7 Tribal Council, the Federation of Saskatchewan Indian Nations and the Banff Bow Valley Task Force. He was awarded the Gustavus Myers Award in 1997, for outstanding work on human rights in North America, for his book *The Spirit and Intent of Treaty 7*. His long poem *Sightings* was nominated for the McNally-Robinson Book of the Year in Manitoba in 1992. A previous volume of poetry, *Where the Land Gets Broken*, received the Stephan G. Stephansson for best poetry book in Alberta in 2005. *Documentaries* is his eighth book of poetry.